D0998920

Soprano
Volume 2

THE
SINGERS
MUSICAL THEATRE
ANTHOLOGY

A collection of songs from the musical stage, categorized by voice type. The selections are presented in their authentic settings, excerpted from the original vocal scores.

Compiled and Edited by Richard Walters

HAL•LEONARD™
CORPORATION

7777 W. BLUEMOUND RD. P.O. BOX 13819 MILWAUKEE, WI 53213

ISBN 0-7935-2329-X

FOREWORD

As the century nears its end, it is apparent to me that the most important and lasting body of performable American music for singers has come from the musical theatre and musical film. The classical tradition as it has been continued in the United States in this century has produced few major composers who have written extensively for the voice, producing a relatively small body of sometimes profound and beautiful literature, but often relevant only to specialized audiences. In pre-rock era popular traditions, the songs that were not written for the stage or film are largely inferior in quality to those written for Broadway and Hollywood (although there are plenty of exceptions to this general rule). Perhaps the reason is simply that the top talent was attracted to and nurtured by those two venues, and inspired by the best performers. But it's also possible that writing for a character playing some sort of scene, no matter how thin the dramatic context (sometimes undetectable), has inherently produced better songs. Compare a Rodgers and Hart ballad from the 1930s (which are all from musicals) to just an average pop ballad from that time not from the stage or screen, if you can dig one up, and you might see what I mean. Popular music of the rock era, primarily performers writing dance music for themselves to record, is almost a completely different aesthetic, and is most often ungratifying for the average singer to present in a typical performance with piano accompaniment.

The five volumes that comprise the original edition of *The Singer's Musical Theatre Anthology,* released in 1987, contain many of the most famous songs for a voice type, as well as being peppered with some more unusual choices. Volume two of the series allows a deeper investigation into the available literature. I have attempted to include a wide range of music, appealing to many different tastes and musical and vocal needs. As in the first volumes, whenever possible the songs are presented in what is their most authentic setting, excerpted from the vocal score or piano/rehearsal score, in the key originally performed and with the original piano accompaniment arrangement (which is really a representation of the orchestra, of course, although Kurt Weill was practically the only Broadway composer to orchestrate his own shows). A student of this subject will notice that these accompaniments are quite a bit different from the standard sheet music arrangements that were published of many of these songs, where the melody is put into a simplified piano part and moved into a convenient and easy piano key, without much regard to vocal range.

In the first volume of the series, I tried to walk a fine line in the mezzo-soprano choices, attempting to accommodate a mix of how theatre people define that voice type —almost exclusively meaning belting — and how classical tradition defines mezzo-soprano. In volume two I have restricted the choices to songs for a belting range, although they don't necessarily need to be belted, and put any songs sung in what theatre people call "head voice" or "soprano voice" in the soprano volume. As was true in the first volume, classically trained mezzo-sopranos will be comfortable with many of the songs in the soprano book.

The "original" keys are presented here, although that often means only the most comfortable key for the original performer. Transpositions of this music are perfectly acceptable. Some songs in these volumes might be successfully sung by any voice type. Classical singers and teachers using these books should remember that the soprano tessitura of this style of material, which often seems very low, was a deliberate aesthetic choice, aimed at clarity of diction, often done to avoid a cultured sound in a singing voice inappropriate to the desired character of the song and role, keeping what I term a Broadway ingenue range. Barbara Cook and Julie Andrews are famous examples of this kind of soprano, with singing concentrated in an expressive and strong middle voice. Also regarding tessituras, some men may find comfortable songs in both the tenor and baritone volumes, in a "baritenor" range, typically with a top note of G.

It's exciting to present songs in this new edition that have never before appeared in print. Many great songs still hold the stage, even if many of the shows don't. The nine volumes of the series present 358 songs from 117 musicals, dating from 1905 to 1991. It's a small percentage of our theatre heritage, but is still a comprehensive and relatively representative sampling of the stage music of New York, and to a much lesser degree London, in the twentieth century.

Many people have been kind and helpful to me in my research and preparation of this edition. They will forgive me if I only mention my debt of gratitude to the late musical theatre historian Stanley Green. I was fortunate enough to work with him as his editor on his last two books. Stanley's grasp of the subject, his compelling prose, and his high standards of research continue to inspire me.

Richard Walters, editor
May, 1993

THE SINGER'S MUSICAL THEATRE ANTHOLOGY
Soprano
Volume 2

Contents

ABOUT THE SHOWS

The material in this section is by Stanley Green and Richard Walters, some of which was previously published elsewhere.

ANYTHING GOES

Music and Lyrics: Cole Porter
Book: Guy Bolton & P.G. Wodehouse, Howard Lindsay & Russel Crouse
Director: Howard Lindsay
Choreographer: Robert Alton
Opened: 11/21/34, New York; a run of 420 performances

Cole Porter's best score of the 1930s is a fun-filled story taking place on an ocean liner about a group of oddball characters, including a nightclub singer, an enamoured stow away, a debutante, and an underworld criminal disguised as a clergyman. Featuring a fresh, young Ethel Meman, the show was one of the biggest hits of its time, containing such hits as the title song, "You're the Top," "I Get a Kick Out of You," "Blow, Gabriel, Blow," and "All Through the Night." *Anything Goes* played Off Broadway in a 1962 production (239 performances), and enjoyed its biggest success in a 1987 Broadway revival starring Patti LuPone (804 performances). There is a 1936 filmed version, and another movie from 1956 with the title *Anything Goes,* but which bears little resemblance to the original. An excellent new recording, faithful to the 1934 original production, was released in the 1980s featuring Frederica Von Stade, Cris Groenendaal, and Kim Griswell.

CONVERSATION PIECE

Music, Lyrics and Book: Noël Coward
Director: Noël Coward
Opened: 1/15/34, London; a run of 177 performances
10/23/34, New York; a run of 55 performances

In *Conversation Piece,* theatregoers were transported back to the fashionable seaside resort of Brighton during the Regency period in England. The stylish operetta was concerned with an impoverished French duke and his attempts to find a suitably wealthy husband for his ward, though eventually the two follow their secret hearts and confess their love for each other. The musical was written expressly for Yvonne Printemps (she sang "I'll Follow My Secret Heart") by the multi-talented Noël Coward, who also played the part of the duke when *Conversation Piece* first opened in London. Most of the original cast was recruited for the New York engagement, except for the substitution of Pierre Fresnay for Mr. Coward.

THE ENCHANTRESS

Music: Victor Herbert
Lyrics and Book: Harry B. Smith
Opened: 10/9/11, Washington, D.C.
12/11, New York

The Irish born Victor Herbert (1859-1924) was the most successful American composer of his time. He and his mother moved to Germany in 1866 when she married a German physician, and he received his musical training in that country, becoming an excellent cellist. Herbert's wife, a soprano, was engaged by the Metropolitan Opera, and he came along to New York, soon to be at the center of the city's musical life as a cellist and conductor. He began composing operettas in 1894, and wrote 40 such works in the next 30 years. The plots of these pieces are formulamatic and often negligible. The only one performed regularly is *Babes in Toyland,* although *The Red Mill* (1906) was successfully revived on Broadway in 1945 and was Herbert's biggest hit in his time.

EVENING PRIMROSE

Music and Lyrics: Stephen Sondheim
Teleplay: James Goldman
Director: Paul Bogart
Telecast on 11/16/66

The short lived ABC series *Stage 67* presented original teleplays, mostly by theatre writers in New York. Based on a John Collier story, *Evening Primrose* is about an poet who hides out in a department store to get away from the world. Much to his surprise, he meets hermits who have been hiding in there for years, and among them is a girl—they fall in love. Most of the music from this show was recorded by Bernadette Peters and Mandy Patinkin on his "Dress Casual" album.

EVITA

Music: Andrew Lloyd Webber
Lyrics: Tim Rice
Director: Harold Prince
Choreographer: Larry Fuller
Opened: 6/23/78, London; a run of 2,900 performances.
       9/25/79, New York; a run of 1,567 performances

Because of its great success in London, *Evita* was practically a pre-sold hit when it began its run on Broadway. Based on the events in the life of Argentina's strong-willed leader, Eva Peron, the musical—with Patti LuPone in the title role in New York—traced her rise from struggling actress to wife of dictator Juan Peron (Bob Gunton), and virtual co-ruler of the country. Part of the concept of the show is to have a slightly misplaced Che Guevera (played by Mandy Patinkin) as a narrator and conscience to the story of Eva's quick, greedy rise to power and her early death from cancer. "Another Suitcase in Another Hall," is a poignant "bimbo" song, sung by Juan Peron's previous and temporary co-habitant upon being kicked out on the street, replaced by Eva.

FIORELLO!

Music: Jerry Bock
Lyrics: Sheldon Harnick
Book: Jerome Weidman and George Abbott
Director: George Abbott
Choreographer: Peter Gennaro
Opened: 11/23/59, New York; a run of 795 performances

New York's favorite mayor, Fiorello LaGuardia, was a peppery, pugnacious reformer whose larger-than-life personality readily lent itself to depiction on the musical stage. With Tom Bosley making an auspicious Broadway debut in the title role, *Fiorello!* covered the ten year period in LaGuardia's life before he became mayor. It begins with his surprise election to congress prior to World War I, and "When Did I Fall in Love" is sung by his adoring wife after he strides off to work at Capitol Hill. *Fiorello!* had the distinction of being the third musical to win the Pulitzer Prize in Drama, joining the ranks of *Of Thee I Sing* and *South Pacific*.

GUYS AND DOLLS

Music and Lyrics: Frank Loesser
Book: Abe Burrows and Jo Swerling
Director: George S. Kaufman
Choreographer: Michael Kidd
Opened: 11/24/50, New York; a run of 1,200 performances

Populated by the hard-shelled but soft-centered characters who inhabit the world of writer Damon Runyon, this "Musical Fable of Broadway" tells the tale of how Miss Sarah Brown of the Save-a-Soul Mission saves the souls of assorted Times Square riff-raff while losing her heart to the smooth-talking gambler, Sky Masterson. "I'll Know" is sung as a duet by Sarah and Sky early in their acquaintance. "If I Were a Bell" shows Sarah under the unfamiliar and, for the moment, giddy effects of alcohol supplied by Sky. An enormously successful revival opened on Broadway in 1992. The 1955 film version stars Frank Sinatra, Marlon Brando, Jean Simmons and Vivian Blaine.

JACQUES BREL IS ALIVE AND WELL AND LIVING IN PARIS

Music: Jacques Brel
Lyrics: Jacques Brel, others (in French); English lyrics by Eric Blau, Mort Schumann
Opened: 1968, New York

A long running intimate Off-Broadway hit, the revue is a collection of some 25 songs by French songwriter Jacques Brel (he wrote both music and lyrics for some, lyrics only for others). The show is conceived for 4 players (2 men, 2 women), and the songs are full of contrasts in subject matter, from the draft, to old age, to bullfights, to death, to love. A film version was released in the early 1970s.

THE KING AND I

Music: Richard Rodgers
Lyrics and Book: Oscar Hammerstein II
Director: John van Bruten
Choreographer: Jerome Robbins
Opened: 3/29/51, New York; a run of 1,246 performances

The idea of turning Margaret Landon's novel *Anna and the King of Siam* into a musical first occurred to Gertrude Lawrence, who saw it as a suitable vehicle for her return to the Broadway musical stage. Based on the diaries of an adventurous Englishwoman, the story is set in Bangkok in the early 1860s. Anna Leonowens, who has accepted the post of schoolteacher to the Siamese king's children, has frequent clashes with the monarch but eventually comes to exert great influence on him, particularly in creating a more democratic society for his people. The show marked the fifth collaboration between Richard Rodgers and Oscar Hammerstein II, and their third to run over one thousand performances.

Cast opposite Miss Lawrence (who died in 1952 during the run of the play) was the then little known Yul Brynner. In 1956 he co-starred with Deborah Kerr in the movie version. In 1992 a new recording starring Julie Andrews and Ben Kingsley was released to mixed reviews. "I Whistle a Happy Tune" is sung at the top of the show by Anna and her young son as a bit of reassurance in arriving alone in a strange land.

KISMET

Music and Lyrics: Robert Wright and George Forrest based on Alexander Borodin
Book: Charles Lederer and Luther Davis
Director: Albert Marre
Choreographer: Jack Cole
Opened: 12/3/53, New York; a run of 583 performances

The story of *Kismet* was adapted from Edward Knoblock's play first presented in New York in 1911 as a vehicle for Otis Skinner. The music of *Kismet* was adapted from themes by Alexander Borodin, from such works as the "Polovitsian Dances" and "In the Steppes of Central Asia." The musical's action occurs within a twenty-four hour period from dawn to dawn, in and around ancient Baghdad, where a Public Poet (first played by Alfred Drake), assumes the identity of Jauu the beggar and gets into all sorts of Arabian Nights adventures. At the end of the day, he is elevated to the position of Emir of Baghdad. His daughter, Marsinah, sings "And This Is My Beloved" to the young Prince Caliph, her new husband. The film version was made by MGM in 1955. A new recording of the musical was released in 1992 with opera star Samuel Ramey in the role of the poet and soprano Ruth Ann Swensen.

KISS ME, KATE

Music and Lyrics: Cole Porter
Book: Samuel and Bella Spewack
Director: John C. Wilson
Choreographer: Hanya Holm
Opened: 12/30/48, New York; a run of 1,077 performances

The genesis of Cole Porter's longest-running musical occurred in 1935 when producer Saint Subber, then a stagehand for the Theatre Guild's production of Shakespeare's *The Taming of the Shrew*, became aware that its stars Alfred Lunt and Lynn Fontanne, quarreled almost as much in private as did the characters in the play. Years later he offered this parallel story as the basis for a musical comedy to the same writing trio, Porter and the Spewacks, who had already worked on the successful show, *Leave It to Me!* The entire action of *Kiss Me, Kate* occurs backstage and onstage at Ford's Theatre, Baltimore, during a tryout of a musical version of *The Taming Of The Shrew*. The main plot concerns the egotistical actor-producer Fred Graham and his temperamental ex-wife Lili Vanessi who —like Shakespeare's Petruchio and Kate— fight and make up and eventually demonstrate their enduring affection for each other. One of the chief features of the score is the skillfull way Cole Porter combined his own musical world (songs like "So in Love," "Too Darn Hot," "Why Can't You Behave?") with a Shakespearean world (songs like "I Hate Men"). In the first brief scene Fred Graham is giving last minute instructions to the cast of the show within a show. He ignores his ex-wife, movie star Lilli Vanessi, who blurts out a response and goes off. Lilli's maid, Hattie, shrugs and sings "Another Op'nin', Another Show." A screen version from MGM was released in 1953.

LITTLE MARY SUNSHINE

Music, Lyrics and Book: Rick Besoyan
Directors: Ray Harrison and Rick Besoyan
Choreographer: Ray Harrison
Opened: 11/18/59, New York (Off Broadway); a run of 1,143 performances

Little Mary Sunshine, a witty, melodious takeoff of the *Naughty Marietta/Rose-Marie/*Jeannette MacDonald-Nelson Eddy school of operetta, was initially presented at a nightclub some three years before the long-running production opened Off Broadway. The story is set in the Colorado Rockies early in the century, and deals with the romance between the mincing heroine and stalwart Captain Big Jim Warrington, who saves his beloved from the clutches of a treacherous Indian just in time for their "Colorado Love Call" duet. "Look for a Sky of Blue" is Mary's entrance number in the show, sung with a pack of admiring but gentlemanly forest rangers.

A LITTLE NIGHT MUSIC

Music and Lyrics: Stephen Sondheim
Book: Hugh Wheeler
Director: Harold Prince
Choreographer: Patricia Birch
Opened: 2/25/73, New York; a run of 601 performances

Based on Ingmar Bergman's 1955 film, *Smiles of a Summer Night,* the score for *A Little Night Music* is composed in 3 (3/4, 3/8, 9/8, etc.), and contains Sondheim's biggest hit song, "Send in the Clowns." The show is a sophisticated, somewhat jaded look at a group of well-to-do Swedes at the turn of the century, among them a lawyer, Fredrik Egerman, his virginal child-bride, Anne, his former mistress, the actress Desirée Armfeldt, Desirée's current lover, the aristocratic Count Carl-Magnus Malcolm, the count's suicidal wife, other guests, and some witty servants. Eventually, the proper partners are sorted out during a weekend party at the country house of Desirée's mother, a former concubine of European nobility. A film version, with a change of locale to Vienna, was released in 1978. "The Glamorous Life," sung by Desirée's daughter, is an ensemble in the show; Sondheim adapted a solo version for the movie that appears in this volume.

MAME

Music and Lyrics: Jerry Herman
Book: Jerome Lawrence and Robert E. Lee
Director: Gene Sachs
Choreographer: Onna White
Opened: 5/24/66, New York; a run of 1,508 performances

Ten years after premiering the comedy based on Patrick Dennis' fictional account of his free-wheeling *Auntie Mame,* playwrights Lawrence and Lee joined forces with Jerry Herman to transform their play into a musical. Angela Lansbury, after years of stage and screen performances, finally achieved her stardom in the title role. In the story, Agnes Gooch, who is part of Mame's domestic staff, has been encouraged by the eccentric lady of the house to go out and *live.* In the late stages of pregnancy she returns to confront her mentor in "Gooch's Song." A 1983 revival, also starring Miss Lansbury, had a brief run on Broadway. A film version, virtually the last old-fashioned musical movie made, was released in 1974, starring Lucille Ball and Robert Preston, and from the original cast, Bea Arthur. The non-musical film of the story, *Auntie Mame,* was released in 1957 and starred Rosalind Russell.

THE MERRY WIDOW

Music: Franz Lehár
Book and Lyrics: Victor Léon and Leo Stein (the original in German)
Opened: 1905, Vienna.
 1906, London (English Lyrics by Adrian Ross); 778 performances
 1907, New York; 416 performances

The epitome of the swirling, melodious, romantic post-Straussian Viennese operetta, *The Merry Widow* was first performed in Vienna as *Die lustige Witwe.* Its initial English-language version ran in London for 778 performances. This was the text that was used for the New York production, which was so acclaimed (a run of a year was an enormous hit in those days) that it even prompted the introduction of Merry Widow hats, gowns, corsets, and cigarettes. The story, based on a French play, *L'Attaché d'Ambassade,* is set in Paris and tells of the efforts of the ambassador of the imaginary kingdom of Marsovia to get his attaché, Prince Danilo, to marry the wealthy widow (named either Hanna or Sonya, depending on the version), so that she might contribute to the tiny country's dwindling finances. Though he balks at being a fortune hunter, Danilo finds himself falling in love and eventually proposes marriage—but only after the young widow has led him to believe that she is penniless. The operetta has had five Broadway revivals, the last and most successful in 1943 for a run of 322 performances, returning to New York after a tour to add another 32 performances. The piece has entered the regular repertories of many opera companies. There have been at least 12 different English versions of the show over the years, including a version by Broadway lyricist Sheldon Harnick.

THE MOST HAPPY FELLA

Music, Lyrics and Book: Frank Loesser
Director: Joseph Anthony
Choreographer: Dania Krupska
Opened: 5/3/56, New York; a run of 676 performances

Adapted from Sidney Howard's Pulitzer Prize-winning play, *They Knew What They Wanted,* Loesser's musical was a particularly ambitious work for the Broadway theatre, with more than thirty separate musical numbers, including arias, duets, trios, quartets, choral pieces, and recitatives. Robust, emotional expressions (such as "Joey, Joey, Joey" and "My Heart Is So Full of You") were interspersed with more traditional specialty numbers (such as "Big D" and "Standing on the Corner"), though in the manner of an opera, the program credits did not list individual selections. In the story, set in California's Napa Valley, an aging vineyard owner (originally played by opera singer Robert Weede) proposes by mail to a waitress he calls Rosabella. She accepts, but is so upset to find Tony old and fat that on their wedding night she allows herself to be seduced by Joe, the handsome ranch foreman. Once he discovers that his wife is to have another man's child, Tony threatens to kill Joe, but there is a reconciliation and the vintner offers to raise the child as his own. A 1979 Broadway revival, starring Giorgio Tozzi, ran for 52 performances. A more successful revival ran in New York in 1991-92, resulting in a new recording of the score.

MY FAIR LADY

Music: Frederick Loewe
Lyrics and Book: Alan Jay Lerner
Director: Moss Hart
Choreographer: Hanya Holm
Opened: 3/15/56, New York; a run of 2,717 performances

The most celebrated musical of the 1950s began as an idea of Hungarian film producer Gabriel Pascal, who devoted the last two years of his life trying to find writers to adapt George Bernard Shaw's play, *Pygmalion,* into a stage musical. The team of Lerner and Loewe also saw the possibilities, particularly when they realized that they could use most of the original dialogue and simply expand the action. They were also scrupulous in maintaining the Shavian flavor in their songs. Shaw's concern with class distinction and his belief that barriers would fall if all Englishmen would learn to speak properly was conveyed through a story about Eliza Doolittle (a star making role for Julie Andrews), a scruffy flower seller in London's Covent Garden, taken on as a speech student of linguistics Professor Henry Higgins (played by Rex Harrison) to increase her social and economic potential. Eliza succeeds so well that she outgrows her social station and even makes Higgins fall in love with her. Though the record was subsequently broken, *My Fair Lady* became the longest running production in Broadway history, remaining for over six and a half years. The show was also a solid success in London. For the 1964 movie version, Julie Andrews was passed over for Audrey Hepburn as Eliza (whose singing was dubbed by Marni Nixon), along with Harrison. Two major revivals have been mounted in New York as of this writing. In 1976 the musical ran for 377 performances with Ian Richardson and Christine Andreas. In 1981 New York again saw Rex Harrison in 119 performances with Nancy Ringham's Eliza. In the late 1980s a new recording of the musical was released with Kiri Te Kanawa and Jeremy Irons in the leading roles.

THE MYSTERY OF EDWIN DROOD

Music, Lyrics and Book: Rupert Holmes
Director: Wilford Leach
Choreographer: Graciela Daniele
Opened: 12/2/85, New York; a run of 608 performances

The Mystery of Edwin Drood came to Broadway after being initially presented the previous summer in a series of free performances sponsored by the New York Shakespeare Festival at the Delacorte Theatre in Central Park. The impressive score was the first stage work of composer-lyricist-librettist Rupert Holmes, who had previously revealed a talent limited to commercial pop. Holmes' lifelong fascination with Charles Dickens' unfinished novel had been the catalyst for the project. Since there were no clues as to Drood's murderer or even if a murder had been committed, Holmes decided to let the audience provide the show's ending by voting how it turns out. The writer's second major decision was to offer the musical as if it were being performed by an acting company at London's Music Hall Royale in 1873. On November 13, 1986, in an attempt to attract more theatre-goers, the musical's title was changed to *Drood.*

NINE

Music and Lyrics: Maury Yeston
Book: Arthur Kopit, Mario Fratti
Director: Tommy Tune
Choreographers: Tommy Tune and Thommie Walsh
Opened: 5/9/82, New York; a run of 732 performances

The influence of the director-choreographer was emphasized again with Tommy Tune's highly stylized, visually striking production of *Nine,* which, besides being a feast for the eyes is also one of the very few non-Sondheim Broadway scores to have true musical substance and merit from the 1970s and 1980s. The musical evolved from Yeston's fascination with Federico Fellini's semi-autobiographical 1963 film *8 1/2.* The story spotlights Guido Contini (played originally by Raul Julia), a celebrated but tormented director who has come to a Venetian spa for a rest, and his relationships with his wife, his mistress, his protégé, his producer, and his mother. The production, which flashes back to Guido's youth and also takes place in his imagination, offers such inventive touches as an overture in which Guido conducts his women as if they were instruments, and an impressionistic version of the Folies Bergères. "A Call from the Vatican" refers to what Guido has told his secretary about a sexy phone call that comes from his mistress. "Unusual Way" is sung to Guido by his young actress protégé. "Simple" is sung by the mistress as Guido's midlife crisis accelerates, and he is temporarily left alone.

110 IN THE SHADE

Music: Harvey Schmidt
Lyrics: Tom Jones
Book: N. Richard Nash
Director: Joseph Anthony
Choreographer: Agnes de Mille
Opened: 10/24/63, New York; 330 performances

N. Richard Nash adapted his own play, *The Rainmaker,* for Schmidt and Jones' first Broadway musical, following their wildly successful *The Fantasticks* Off-Broadway. Nash's play is probably best remembered for the film version which starred Burt Lancaster and Katharine Hepburn. It is a simple tale of Lizzie, an aging unmarried woman who lives with her father and brothers on a drought-stricken ranch in the American west. Starbuck, a transient "rainmaker" comes on the scene and is soon seen to be the con man that he is, despite his dazzling charisma. He does, however, pay somewhat sincere attention to Lizzie, and awakens love and life in her. Nevertheless, she sees no future with Starbuck, and winds up with a reliable local suitor instead. Inga Swenson was the musical's original Lizzie, with Robert Horton as Starbuck. The show was featured in a prominent production by New York City Opera in 1992.

PAL JOEY

Music: Richard Rodgers
Lyrics: Lorenz Hart
Book: John O'Hara
Director: George Abbott
Choreographer: Robert Alton
Opened: 12/25/40, New York; a run of 374 performances

With its heel for a hero, its smoky night-club atmosphere, and its true-to-life characters, *Pal Joey* was a major breakthrough in bringing about a more adult form of musical theatre. Adapted by John O'Hara from his own New Yorker short stories, the show is about Joey Evans (played by Gene Kelly in his only major Broadway role), an entertainer at a small Chicago night club, who is attracted to the innocent Linda English, but drops her in favor of wealthy, middle-aged Vera Simpson. Vera builds a glittering nightclub for the gigolo, Chez Joey, but she soon grows tired of him. Joey, at the end, is on his way to other conquests. Though it had a respectable run, *Pal Joey* was considered somewhat ahead of its time. A 1952 Broadway revival, with Vivienne Segal repeating her role of Vera, received a more appreciative reception and ran 542 performances. The 1957 film version starred Frank Sinatra, Rita Hayworth and Kim Novak.

PHANTOM

Music and Lyrics: Maury Yeston
Book: Arthur Kopit

Though at this writing Yeston's *Phantom* has not had a Broadway run, it has played widely in the United States, receiving raves from critics in Chicago, Boston, New York, Dallas, and other places. Based on the 1911 French novel, the show's principal characters are Christine and Phantom, and his protective love for her. Yeston and Kopit actually wrote their show before Lloyd Webber wrote his, but were unable to get any financing for a Broadway production after the new British musical was announced. *Phantom* was first seen in Houston in 1991. Among the show's strong score, "This Place Is Mine" is Carlotta's comic song about the opera house where she reigns. Yeston, composer of *Nine* and *Grand Hotel,* is certainly one of the most interesting composers to hit Broadway, with his background as a music textbook author and professor at Yale, and his compositional abilities, further represented by a cello concerto written for Yo-Yo Ma. He wrote the words and music for a song cycle called *December Songs,* commissioned for the Carnegie Hall centennial celebration.

PHILEMON

Music: Harvey Schmidt
Words: Tom Jones
Opened: 1970, New York

The 60s had *The Fantasticks, 110 in the Shade, I Do! I Do!,* and *Celebration* from Schmidt and Jones. Following those shows, the pair developed their own theatre workshop in New York called Portfolio, and in the spirit of that time concentrated on small scale, experimental musicals. *Philemon* was the most notable show to come out of the workshop, and won the Outer Critics Circle Award.

PINS AND NEEDLES

Music and Lyrics: Harold Rome
Book: Sketches by Charles Friedman, Arthur Arent, Marc Blitzstein, Emanuel Eisenberg, David Gregory
Director: Charles Friedman
Choreographer: Gluck Sandor
Opened: 11/27/37, New York; a run of 1,108 performances

Pins and Needles was one of Broadway's most surprising success stories. Initially presented as a satirical revue by and for the members of the International Ladies Garment Workers Union, it was not even covered by critics when it began its run at the tiny Labor Stage (formerly Princess Theatre). But audiences soon began flocking to it in such droves that the show went on to achieve the record as Broadway's longest running musical (though that distinction would soon be relinquished to *Hellzapoppin*). The revue's barbs may have been aimed at militarists, bigots, reactionaries, Nazis, Fascists, Communists, and the Daughters of the American Revolution, but the tone was generally lighthearted, with even the demand of "Sing Me a Song With Social Significance" done with tongue in cheek. To keep up with the headlines, so much material had to be constantly changed that by 1939 the show was called *New Pins and Needles.*

THE PIRATES OF PENZANCE

Music: Arthur Sullivan
Libretto: W. S. Gilbert
Opened: December 30, 1879, Paignton, England

Gilbert and Sullivan operettas were the hottest musical theatre around in the 1870s and 1880s in both England and the U.S. 1878 saw the hugely successful premiere of HMS Pinafore, so when *The Pirates of Penzance* debuted in 1879, there was a theatre public clamoring for tickets. The show opened in New York one day later than in England. On the rocky coast of Cornwall, Frederick has abandoned his pirate shipmates and plans to return to civilization. He stumbles on a group of girls getting ready to bathe in the ocean, and scares them into a panic. The star of the show, Mabel, calms all with her aria "Poor Wand'ring One," and her companions wonder aloud if she would have been so charitable if Frederick had not been so handsome. The show was successfully produced on Broadway in 1981 with a cast that included Linda Ronstadt, Rex Smith, Kevin Kline, George Rose and Estelle Parsons. A movie version was made of the production with the Broadway cast, and with Angela Lansbury.

PLAIN AND FANCY

Music: Albert Hague
Lyrics: Arnold B. Horwitt
Book: Joseph Stein and Will Glickman
Director: Morton Da Costa
Choreographer: Helen Tamiris
Opened: 1/27/55, New York; a run of 461 performances

The setting of *Plain and Fancy* was Amish country in Pennsylvania, where two worldly New Yorkers (Richard Derr and Shirl Conway) have gone to sell a farm they inherited—but not before they had a chance to meet the God-fearing people and appreciate their simple but unyielding way of living. The warm and atmospheric score, with its hit song "Young and Foolish" was composed by Albert Hague, familiar to television viewers as the bearded music teacher in the series Fame. *Plain and Fancy* was another Barbara Cook show that helped to establish her as Broadway's favorite golden-throated ingenue.

REGINA

Words and Music: Marc Blitzstein
Director: Robert Lewis
Opened: 10/31/49, New York; a run of 56 performances

Regina is among the most distinguished and thrilling American scores for the stage, and in a style that combines a theatrical popularity and serious composition. Gershwin had tried opera on Broadway in 1935 with *Porgy and Bess*—the idea was ahead of its time, but had a great effect on composers to come. By the late 1940s to the early 1950s, there was a small but important trend toward a more grown-up, musically ambitious, serious lyric theatre for Broadway, with Gian Carlo Menotti, Kurt Weill, Marc Blitzstein the prime contributors. *Regina* is based on the Lillian Hellman 1939 play *The Little Foxes* (released as a film with Bette Davis in the title role). "What Will It Be for Me?" is the song of Regina's 17 year old daughter, Alexandra, a good-natured, innocent girl whose character is in sharp contrast to her mother.

THE SECRET GARDEN

Music: Lucy Simon
Lyrics and Book: Marsha Norman
Director: Susan H. Schulman
Choreographer: Michael Lichtefeld
Opened: 4/25/91, New York; 706 performances

Based on the novel by Frances Hodgson Burnett, the story is of an orphaned Mary Lennox, who is sent to live with her uncle Archibald in Yorkshire. He is absorbed in grief over the death of his young wife 10 years earlier, and the house is gloomy and mysterious. Mary finds her dead aunt's "secret garden," passionately nurtures it to life, and Archie also comes back to life once he can let go of his grief. "How Could I Ever Know?" is sung by the ghost of his dead wife, Lilly.

SHE LOVES ME

Music: Jerry Bock
Lyrics: Sheldon Harnick
Book: Joe Masteroff
Director: Harold Prince
Choreographer: Carol Haney
Opened: 4/23/63, New York; a run of 301 performances

The closely integrated, melody drenched score of *She Loves Me* is certainly one of the best ever written for a musical comedy. It was based on a Hungarian play, *Parfumerie*, by Miklos Laszlo, that had already been used as the basis for two films, *The Shop Around the Corner* and *In the Good Old Summertime* (with the setting changed to America). Set in the 1930s in Budapest, the tale is of the people who work in Maraczek's Parfumerie, principally the constantly quibbling sales clerk Amalia Balash (Barbara Cook) and the manager Georg Nowack (Daniel Massey). It is soon revealed that they are anonymous pen pals who agree to meet one night at the Café Imperiale, though neither knows the other's identity. Georg realizes that it is Amalia who is waiting for him in the restaurant, but doesn't let on, leaving her to sit there for hours, culminating in the pleaful "Dear Friend." After she calls in sick their relationship blossoms into love when Georg brings her ice cream; eventually, he is emboldened to reveal his identity by quoting from one of Amalia's letters. *She Loves Me*, which would have starred Julie Andrews had she not been filming *Mary Poppins*, was one of Barbara Cook's most magical portrayals. The show is well represented on the original cast album, which on two disks preserves practically every note of the show's music.

ALL THROUGH THE NIGHT

from *Anything Goes*

Words and Music by
COLE PORTER

close to me. _____ All _____ through the

night, _____ un - der bright _____ stars a - bove _____

_____ You _____ and your love _____ will bring

ec - sta - sy. _____ When dawn's

_____ o - ver - tak - en us, we'll sad - ly say good-

GYPSY IN ME

from *Anything Goes*

Words and Music by
COLE PORTER

Rubato

HOPE:

Long, long a-go, _____ so long a-go I hard-ly know when _____ My great, great Grand-mo-ther now and then stopped _____ with a gyp - sy. The u-sual a-li-bi — a lit-tle bit tip - sy, _____

Tip - sy no, no, _____ of their love there was - n't a doubt _____ So I can't

wait to get the stage all set, So I can let _____ the gyp - sy in me

(rit.)

[Moderato]   Refrain

a tempo   *stacc.*

out. _____   Hid - ing a - way, _____

_____ There's a lit - tle bit of gyp - sy in _ me _____ That's nev - er been

found._____ Wait - ing its day _____

___ There's a lit - tle bit of gyp - sy in __ me _____ Just hang - ing a - round,_

_____ Till the mag - i - cal night _____

___ When the stars by their light give mys - ter - y _____ to the sleep - ing la -

At the mo-ment su - preme

will be shown the un - known   gyp - sy in   me.

I'LL FOLLOW MY SECRET HEART

from *Conversation Piece*

Words and Music by
NOËL COWARD

ART IS CALLING FOR ME

from *The Enchantress*

(The Prima Donna Song)

(1911)

Music by VICTOR HERBERT
Lyrics by HARRY B. SMITH

op - 'ra by Sig - nor Puc - ci - ni. I've rou -
op - 'ra so charm - ing by Gou - nod. Girls would

Poco meno

turn
(tr)

lades and the trills that would send the cold chills down the
be on the brink of hys - ter - ics, I think, e - ven

8va
tr

f Poco meno

ff

8va

Start tr slowly

ff Pesante

(tr) *(ad lib.)*

backs of all hear - ers of my vo - cal frills. _____
strong men would have to go out for a drink. _____

ff

colla voce

mf dim

REFRAIN:

f

I long to be a pri - ma
I long to be a pri - ma

f

fp

32

peach - y can - ta - *tri - ce,   like   oth - er **plump girls that I
"Vi - va" to the di - va,   oh,   ver - y love - ly that must

see; _____ I hate so -
be; _____ That's what I'm

ci - e - ty;   I hate pro - pri - e - ty;
dy - ing for,   That's what I'm sigh - ing for,

(D.C.)

Art is call - ing for me. _____
Art is call - ing for me. _____

* treechy
** optional lyric: "Songbirds" replacing "plump girls"

TAKE ME TO THE WORLD

from *Evening Primrose*

Words and Music by
STEPHEN SONDHEIM

Moderato ma poco rubato (♩ = 80)

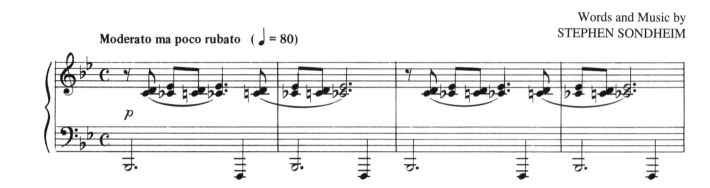

Let me see the world _____ with clouds, Take me to the world. _____

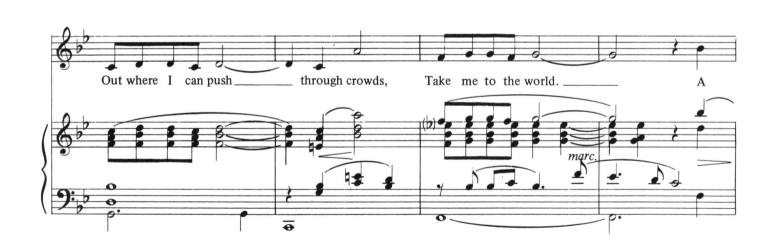

Out where I can push _____ through crowds, Take me to the world. _____ A

hold my hand When-ev-er we ar-rive.

Take me to the world Where I can be a-live!

Let me see the world _____ that smiles,

Take me to the world. _____ Some-where I can walk _____ for miles,

ANOTHER SUITCASE
IN ANOTHER HALL

from *Evita*

Lyrics by TIM RICE
Music by ANDREW LLOYD WEBBER

*It would be stylistically appropriate for the pianist to improvise an accompaniment.

MCA music publishing

40

all the same I hate it, would-n't you? So what hap-pens now? So what hap-pens

**An-oth-er suit-case in an-oth-er hall.

C/G   F   C   F/G   C

now? Where am I go-ing to? _____ Where am I

Take your pic-ture off an-oth-er wall. _ You'll get by, you al-ways have be-fore. _

F/G   C   F   Am

go-ing to?

F C/E Dm   C   F/C C7   F/C   C

**Sung as a chorus by other characters.

WHEN DID I FALL IN LOVE?

from *Fiorello*

Lyrics by SHELDON HARNICK
Music by JERRY BOCK

THEA:
There he goes, my con-gress-man. Start-ing his day hur-ry-ing right ___ to a fight. ___ There he goes Sir

Gal-a-had gal-lo-ping off rid-ing his white ___ Wil-lie's knight.

Out of the house ten sec-onds and I miss him, _____ I miss him more

with each good - bye. Out of the house ten sec - onds and I miss him,

and no one's more as - ton-ished than I. I nev - er

Rubato

once pre - tend-ed that I loved him; ___ when did I start this change of

Slowly and Tenderly

heart?_____ When did I fall in love? What night? Which day?

When did I first be - gin to feel this way?_____ How could the

mo - ment pass, un - felt, ig - nored? Where was the blind - ing flash?

Where was the crash - ing chord? When did I fall in love? I can't_____

I'LL KNOW

from *Guys and Dolls*

Lyrics and Music by
FRANK LOESSER

Slow

SARAH:

I'll know when my love comes a-long, I won't take a chance. For oh he'll be just what I need, not some fly-by-night Broad-way ro-mance. I'll know by the calm stead-y voice, those feet on the ground _____ I'll know as I

*Adapted as a solo here, the song is a
duet scene for Sarah and Sky in the show.*

52

IF I WERE A BELL

from *Guys and Dolls*

Words and Music by
FRANK LOESSER

54

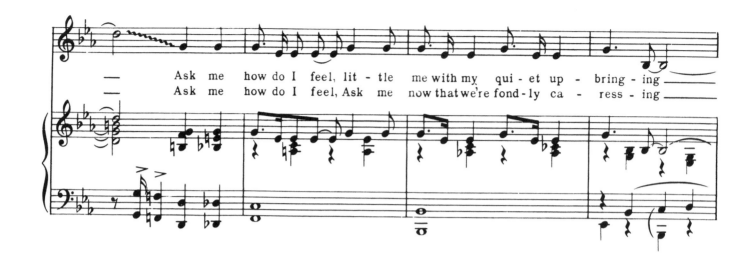

Ask me how do I feel, lit - tle me with my qui - et up - bring - ing
Ask me how do I feel, Ask me now that we're fond - ly ca - ress - ing

Well, sir all I can say is, If I were a gate I'd be swing - ing
(Spoken) Pal, if I were a sal - ad I know I'd be splashing my dress - ing

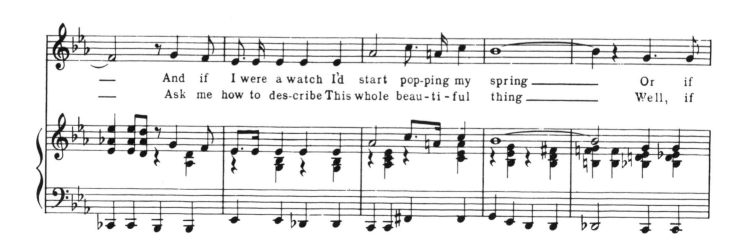

And if I were a watch I'd start pop-ping my spring Or if
Ask me how to des-cribe This whole beau-ti-ful thing Well, if

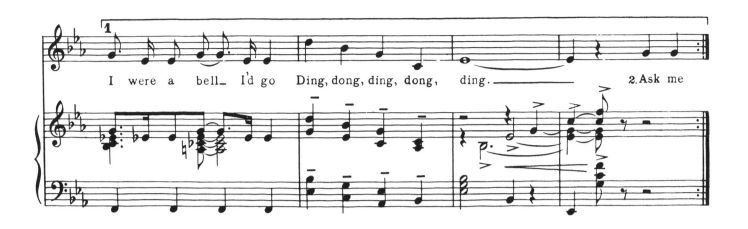

I were a bell_ I'd go Ding, dong, ding, dong, ding._____ 2.Ask me

I were a bell— I'd go ding, dong, ding, dong,

ding._____

I LOVED

from *Jacques Brel Is Alive and Well and Living In Paris*

Original French Words by JACQUES BREL
English Words by MORT SHUMAN and ERIC BLAU
Music by GÉRARD JOVANNEST and FRANÇOIS RAUBER

Poco meno mosso

I loved the towns where we made love, And the ho -

tels where we played games;

I WHISTLE A HAPPY TUNE

from *The King and I*

Lyrics by OSCAR HAMMERSTEIN II
Music by RICHARD RODGERS

[Moderato]

64

You may be as brave as you make be - lieve you

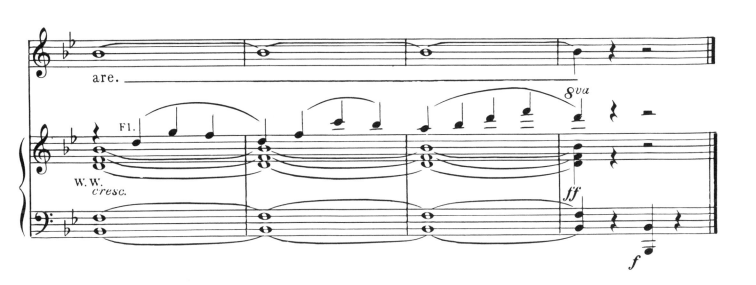

are.

LOOK FOR A SKY OF BLUE

from *Little Mary Sunshine*

Music and Lyrics by
RICK BESOYAN

68

69

AND THIS IS MY BELOVED

from *Kismet*

Music and Lyrics by
ROBERT WRIGHT and GEORGE FORREST
(based on themes of Alexander Borodin)

71

Poco stentato

THE GLAMOROUS LIFE

from *A Little Night Music*

Music and Lyrics by
STEPHEN SONDHEIM

The song appears in a different form in the show.

Mend the clothes and tend the child - ren. Or - din-ar - y moth - ers, like

or - din- ar - y wives, Make the beds and

bake the pies and with - er on the vine. Not

glam - or - ous life! _____

Or - din - ar - y moth-ers nev - er get the flow - ers and

Or - din - ar - y moth-ers nev - er get the joys.

Or - din - ar - y moth-ers could - n't cough for ho - urs, main-

tain - ing their poise.

Sand - wich - es on - ly, but she eats what she

wants when she wants.

Some - times it's lone - ly, _____ but she meets man - y

82

84

hear.
But it does in - ter-
fere
With a gla - mor - ous...
L'istesso tempo
mp
I am the prin - cess, Guard - ed by drag - ons,
sim.
Snort - ing and grumb - ling and rumb - ling in wag - ons.

She's in her king - dom, Wear - ing dis-

guis - es, Liv - ing a life that is full of sur-

pris - es.

p

And

cresc.

cresc. poco a poco

some - time this sum - mer she'll come gal - lop - ing

sub. p cresc. poco a poco *simile*

VILIA

from *The Merry Widow*

(Die Lustige Witwe)

Words by
Viktor Leon and Leo Stein
English Version by Martha Gerhart

Music by
Franz Lehár

HANNA:

Nun lasst uns a - ber wie da - heim jetzt
Now gath - er as we've done be - fore to

sin - gen un - sern Rin - gel reim von ei - ner Fee, die wie be - kannt, da - heim die
sing our fa - v'rite song of yore a - bout a maid of wide-spread fame; you know that

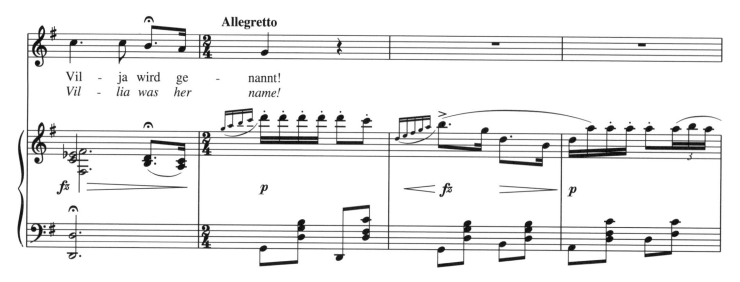

Vil - ja wird ge - nannt!
Vil - lia was her name!

an? Bang fleht ein lieb - kran - ker Mann!_____
why, in your em - bra - ces, I die!_____

ppp (opt. 2nd time)

Vil - ja, o Vil - ja, was thust Du mir
Vi - lia, oh Vi - lia, will love tell me

an?
why,

Bang fleht ein lieb - kran - ker Mann!
in your em - bra - ces, I die!

Allegretto

2. Das Mann!
2. *The die!*

Bang fleht ein lieb -
In your em - bra -

kran - ker Mann!
ces I die!

GOOCH'S SONG
from *Mame*

Music and Lyric by
JERRY HERMAN

With my wings res-o-lute-ly spread, Mis-sis Burn-side, And my old in-hi-bi-tions shed, Mis-sis Burn-side, I did each lit-tle thing you said, Mis-sis Burn-side. I lived! I lived! I lived! I

thanks for the train-ing Now I'm not com-plain-ing, But

you left some-thing out!_____ *Freely* In-stead of

wan-d'ring on with my lone re-morse, I have come back home to com-plete the course. Oh,

Br. Muted

Str. (cued for W.W.)

+W.W.

Tempo I°

What do I do ---

W.W., Str.

Br.

WARM ALL OVER

from *The Most Happy Fella*

Music and Lyrics by
FRANK LOESSER

smile you get me warm all o - ver. Some - times I

feel kind of out in the cold, But then I touch your

hand _____ and I'm home, home a - gain and warm all

o - ver, _____ warm all o - ver. Gone are all the

clouds that used to swarm all o - ver. Please al - ways

let me keep feel-ing the way I do, so warm all

o - ver with a ten - der love for

you.

WITHOUT YOU

from *My Fair Lady*

Lyrics by ALAN JAY LERNER
Music by FREDERICK LOEWE

Allegro con anima

ELIZA:

What a fool I was! What a dom-in-at-ed fool! To think you were the earth and

sky. What a fool I was! What an ad-dle-pat-ed fool! What a

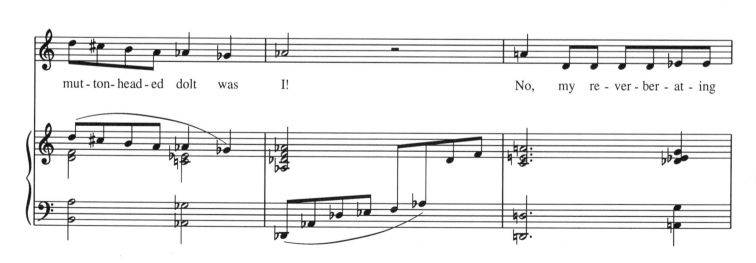

mut-ton-head-ed dolt was I! No, my re-ver-ber-at-ing

well, you can go to Hart-ford, Her-es-ford and Hamp-shire. __ They can still rule the land with-out you. _____ Wind-sor Cas-tle will stand with-out you. _____ And with-out much a-do we can all mud-dle through with-out you.

Poco meno

With-out your pull-ing it, the tide comes in; with-

out your twirl-ing it, the earth can spin. With - out your push-ing them, the clouds roll by. If

Tempo giusto   **Tempo I**

they can do with-out you, duck-y, so can I! I shall not feel a - lone with-out

you. I can stand on my own with-out you. _____ So go

back in your shell, I can do blood-y well with-out you! _____

MOONFALL
from *The Mystery of Edwin Drood*

Words and Music by
RUPERT HOLMES

112

ROSA'S CONFESSION

from *The Mystery of Edwin Drood*

Words and Music by
RUPERT HOLMES

calm - ly plan to kill a man and feel but on - ly glad! To rid her - self— to bid her - self a

mur - der - ous good - bye! Not Ed - win who I sought, but *you*, I

meant for *you* to die!

But the night was far from bright, thick with wet and thun - der. Thatch - ing fell dis - patched from hell!

Is it yet a won - der? Could not see the arms of me stretched out with scarf in hand.

Saw your coat and tied Ned's throat just like a dead - ly wed - ding band!

Faster

So long a time they've thought that I'm a Dres - den

doll, quite na - ive. But I be - lieve this pain, my brain more

Slower

tor - tured than they might con - ceive. With these late ad - di - tions, I have now re - vealed

mur - der - ous ad - mis - sions hith - er - to con - cealed. Damn you all, I say! You

let him drive me mad! Mad - ness led to this, no good can come from bad, no

good — no good can come from bad!! _____

A CALL FROM THE VATICAN
from *Nine*

Lyrics and Music by
MAURY YESTON

Note: *Most of this song is belted.*

UNUSUAL WAY
(IN A VERY UNUSUAL WAY)

from *Nine*

Lyrics and Music by
MAURY YESTON

In a

ver-y un-u-su-al way   one time I need-ed you.
ver-y un-u-su-al way   I think I'm in love with you.

In a
In a

ver-y un-u-su-al way   you were my friend.
ver-y un-u-su-al way   I want to cry.

SIMPLE
from *Nine*

Lyrics and Music by
MAURY YESTON

RAUNCHY
from *110 in the Shade*

Lyrics by TOM JONES
Music by HARVEY SCHMIDT

132

Wear - in' May - bell - ine!___ I'll be so raunch - y, Gon - na make them

oth - er gals turn green. Honk - y tonk - in' ev - 'ry night._ I'm a

raunch - y kind of gal. ___ I'll be so raunch - y, Sip - pin' Doc - tor

Pep - per mixed with booze. Burn - in' like a fuse.

Shak - in' my ca - boose. __ I'll be so raunch - y,

Step-pin' in my pa - tent leath - er shoes. __ (Spoken) When the

cow - boys see me strut __ my stuff, __ gon - na crawl right on their

haunch - es, 'cause they just can't seem to get __ e - nough, I'm a

IS IT REALLY ME?

from *110 in the Shade*

Lyrics by TOM JONES
Music by HARVEY SCHMIDT

SIMPLE LITTLE THINGS

from *110 in the Shade*

Lyrics by TOM JONES
Music by HARVEY SCHMIDT

dreams, like my name, are ver-y plain; no shin-ing knight must kneel. My

dreams, like my name, are ver-y plain; but nev - er-the-less, they're

real. They're all so ver - y real.

142

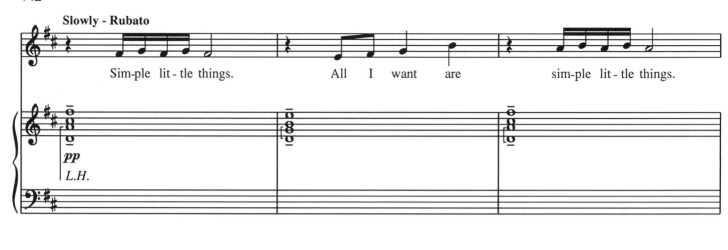

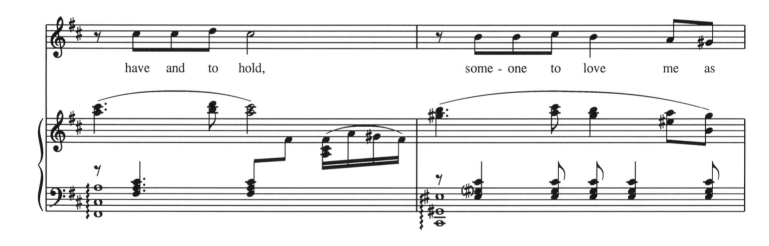

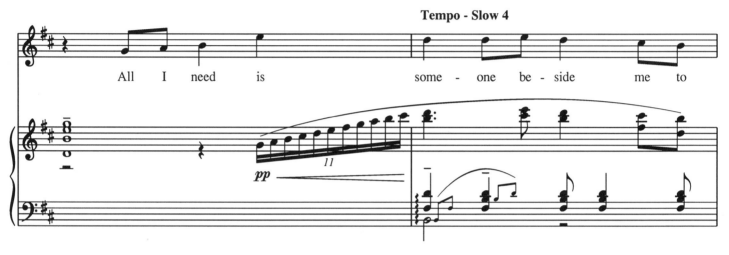

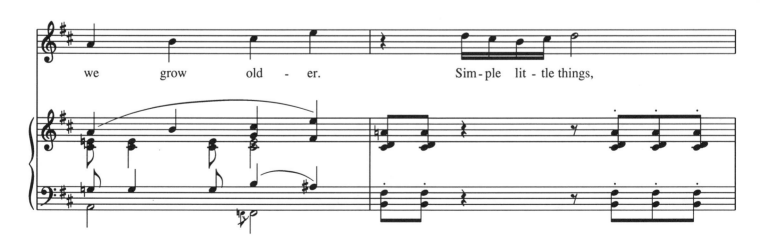

a tempo

Sim-ple lit-tle things. All I want are sim-ple lit-tle things.

All I need is some-one be-side me to _____ have and to hold,

some-one to love me as we grow old - er. Sim-ple lit-tle things, _____

ten. **Very slow - In 8**

___ sim-ple lit-tle dreams, will do.

8va

p

rit.

Ped.

THIS PLACE IS MINE

from *Phantom*

Words and Music by
MAURY YESTON

146

MY TRUE LOVE

from *Phantom*

Words and Music by
MAURY YESTON

Medium Waltz ♩ = 96

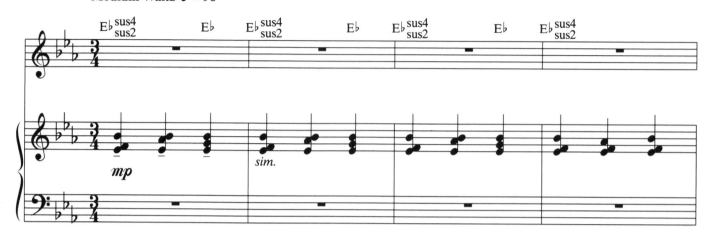

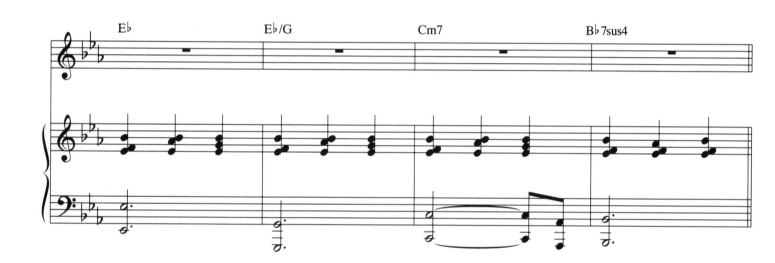

My true love, lost in a
No, my love, more than a

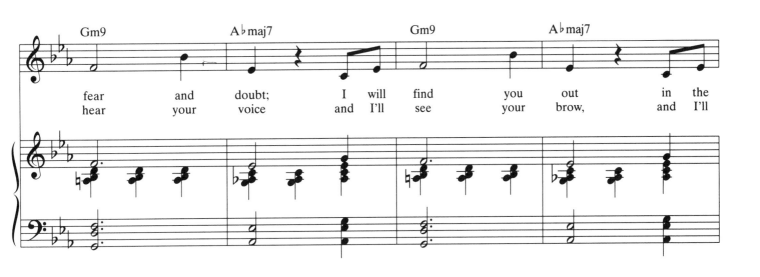

face, like your mu - sic. Can_____ you

hear_____ me now? Can we

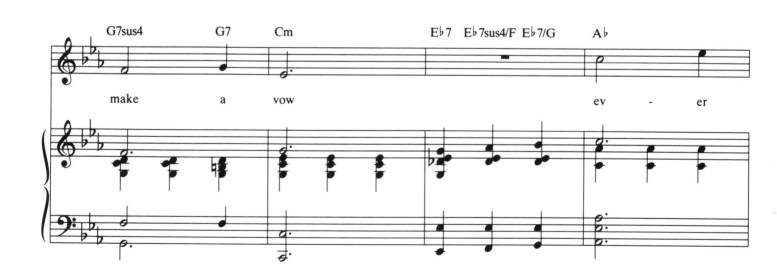

make a vow ev - er

ANOTHER OP'NIN', ANOTHER SHOW

from *Kiss Me, Kate*

Words and Music by
COLE PORTER

Very lively

HATTIE:

An -

162

Four weeks __ you re - hearse and re - hearse. __

Three weeks __ and it could - n't be worse. __

One week, __ will it ev - er be right? __ Then

out of the hat __ it's that big first night! __ The

POOR WAND'RING ONE

from *Pirates of Penzance*

Words by WILLIAM SCHWENK GILBERT

Music by ARTHUR SULLIVAN

can help thee find True peace of mind, Why take_ it, it ___ is

thine! Take heart, no dan - ger lowers;

Take a - ny heart _ but ours! Take heart,

fair days will shine; _ Take a - ny heart, take mine!

WHAT IS A MAN?
from *Pal Joey*

Words by LORENZ HART
Music by RICHARD RODGERS

much too used to love to be with - out it. What is a

man? Is he an an - i - mal? Is he a wolf,

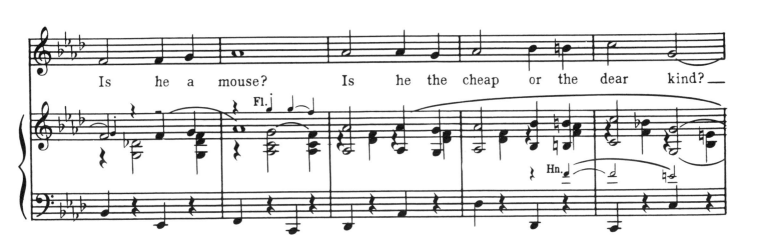

Is he a mouse? Is he the cheap or the dear kind?

Is he cham - pagne or the beer kind? ___

poco rall.

What is a man? Is he a stim - u - lant? Good for the

a tempo

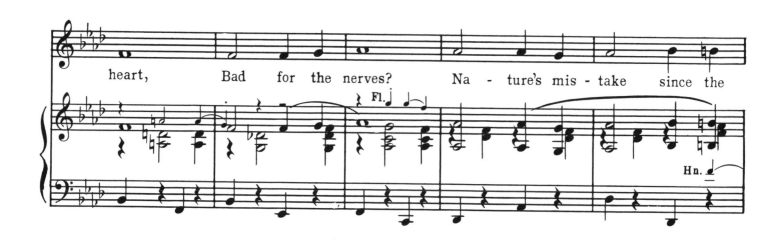

heart, Bad for the nerves? Na - ture's mis - take since the

THE GREATEST OF THESE

from *Philemon*

Lyrics by TOM JONES
Music by HARVEY SCHMIDT

NOBODY MAKES A PASS AT ME

from *Pins and Needles*

Words and Music by
HAROLD ROME

WHAT WILL IT BE FOR ME?

from *Regina*

Words and Music by
MARC BLITZSTEIN

Alexandra:

What will it be for me? Will some-one say "I love you"?

What will it be, to be the one to say "I love you"?

Will it be all real and right? _____ And how will it feel to

real - ly love a per - fect stran - ger? Look in his eyes, and look, and

kiss that per - fect stran - ger? I can not i - mag - ine it quite. It's like

noth - ing else be - fore, The op - en-ing of a door to the light. I

stand at the door, and wait, And won - der who'll come knock - ing.

189

THIS IS ALL VERY NEW TO ME

from *Plain and Fancy*

Lyrics by ARNOLD B. HORWITT
Music by ALBERT HAGUE

Slowly (in 3)

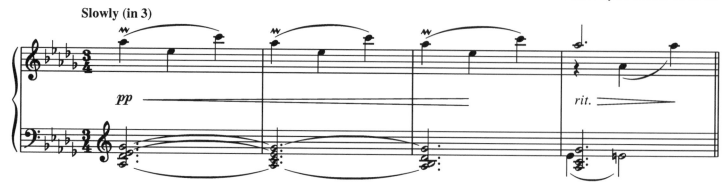

Valse moderato (in 1)

HILDA:

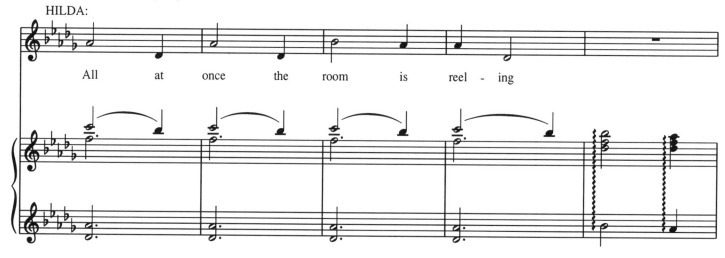

All at once the room is reel - ing

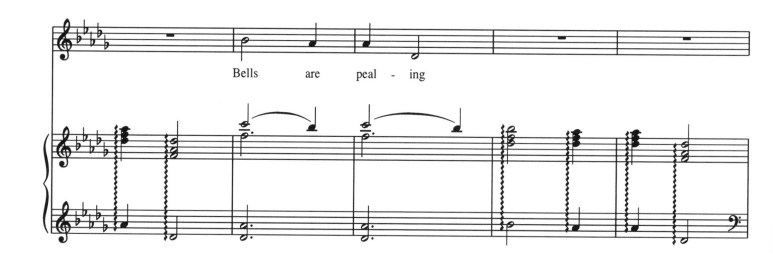

Bells are peal - ing

191

ritenuto *a tempo*

This is all ve - ry new to me _____

mp *ritenuto* *a tempo*

This is all ve - ry fine _____ This so

sun - ny - like, _____ Sort of fun - ny - like, _____ Milk - and -

hon - ey - like feel - ing of mine. _____

193

Scared to death. _____ Are you

won - der - ing why? _____ It's as sim - ple as

Bright Waltz

pie. _____

praise._____

This is all ve - ry

new to me,_____

And I'm knock - ing on

wood._____

What to do?_____

____ What to say?_____

How to make it go

FOLLOW YOUR HEART
from *Plain and Fancy*

Lyrics by ARNOLD B. HORWITT
Music by ALBERT HAGUE

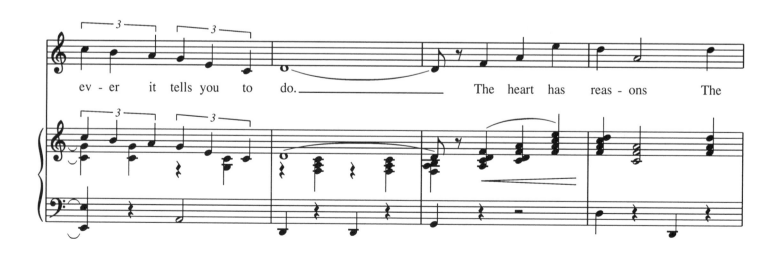

IT WONDERS ME

from *Plain and Fancy*

Lyrics by ARNOLD B. HORWITT
Music by ALBERT HAGUE

205

So won- der -ful sweet _____ the mel - o - dy, _____

It won - ders me. _____ So green the field, _____

So blue the sky, _____ So gold the tree, _____

It won - ders me. _____

HOW COULD I EVER KNOW?
from *The Secret Garden*

Lyrics by MARSHA NORMAN
Music by LUCY SIMON

need me so? How____ can I say not to dream a-bout me?

How_____ could I ev - er know? How____ could I ev - er

Più mosso

know? For - give me, can you for - give me, and

hold me in your heart? And find some new way to

I DON'T KNOW HIS NAME

from *She Loves Me*

Lyrics by SHELDON HARNICK
Music by JERRY BOCK

I don't know his name or what he looks like, But I have a much more cer - tain guide, I can tell ex - act - ly what he looks like in - side._____ _____ When I un-der-took this cor - res - pond - ence, lit-tle did I know I'd grow so

fond. Lit-tle did I know our views would so cor - res - pond. _____

_____ He writes me what his feel - ings are on Shaw, Flau-bert, Cho-

sim.

pin, Ren-oir; The more I read the more I find we're one in mind and

cresc.

heart. I know the kind of home we'd share, the books, the prints, the

sim.

mu - - sic there. A home, a life, that's warm and full and rich in love and

art. _____ I don't need to see his hand-some pro - file I don't need to

see his man - ly frame. All I need to know is in each let - ter. Each long re - veal-ing

let-ter. I could-n't know him bet - ter if I knew his name.

rall.

Broader

ad lib.

colla voce

WILL HE LIKE ME?

from *She Loves Me*

Lyrics by SHELDON HARNICK
Music by JERRY BOCK

215

lone and I write _____

Thoughts come eas - i - ly, words come flu - ent - ly then. _____

rit.

That's how it is when I'm a - lone, but to -

Press forward

night _____ There's no hid - ing be - hind my pa - per and

cresc.

DEAR FRIEND

from *She Loves Me*

Lyrics by SHELDON HARNICK
Music by JERRY BOCK

Poignantly (slowly)

Charm - ing, ro - man - tic, the per - fect ca - fè.

Then as if it is - n't bad e - nough, a vi - o - lin starts to play.

Can - dles and wine, tab - les for two,

but where are you, dear friend?

cou - ples go past me, I see how they look.

So dis - creet-ly sym - pa - thet - ic when they see the rose and the book.

I make be - lieve, noth - ing is wrong.

How long can I pre - tend?_____

please make it right. don't break my heart.

Don't let it end, dear friend.